In this heart-warming short book Isabel and Oliver have shared their story openly and honestly. Their conviction is that the best way to approach life's ups and downs is in a relationship with Jesus Christ. They show how their story makes most sense when seen as part of a bigger, better story – God's story. Aspects of the Bible narrative we know quite well about the birth of Jesus are weaved into the nitty gritty of Isabel's cancer diagnosis and their reactions that follow. This book will be helpful to many because it deals with life's challenges while maintaining a joyful perspective. The courage they have displayed in writing of their experience is inspiring.

Elaine Duncan, Chief Executive, Scottish Bible Society

An indescribably poignant and raw illustration of the last days of a life lived to full in the shadow of death. Written by two newly-weds, whose time is cut short by cancer, this book could have been about fractured dreams but instead is a powerful testament to the beauty of faith in the midst of pain and grief, and a reminder of the preciousness of time spent with those we love – and of God's unending love. A great gift to those left behind.

Kate Nicholas, author, broadcaster, blogger and preacher

This is a remarkable and deeply moving book which is a tribute to a profound human love, but far more than that: it is a spiritual adventure story. Anyone who reads this with an open heart will be touched and inspired because this is about living well and dying well, it is about comfort and hope amid the overwhelming challenges of cancer and COVID-19. It is about divine transformation. Oliver and Isabel depict a world where a parking place in a hospital car park can become 'holy ground', a sacred space of heartfelt prayer, where three brief years of a marriage afflicted by a deadly disease can become a threshold to eternity.

Woven through this account of human tears and tragedy and hope, told with such honesty and humility, there is the timeless beauty of the Christmas story. It is an original and surprising approach to the ancient theme of suffering, enriched by poems, hymns and songs – and above all by the shining witness of two people on the ultimate journey of faith.

Murray Watts, playwright, author and
director of The Wayfarer Trust

D1342819

Cancer and Christmas are not two words that sit easily together, yet in this book Oliver and Isabel Vellacott help us see how the love that came down at Christmas is the love that can carry us through the most challenging of circumstances.

Isabel shares how she was given a Stage 4 diagnosis of cancer just days before her retirement, and only months after being married to Oliver, yet found the grace to bear her suffering without bitterness or self-pity.

Oliver helps us understand from Scripture how we too may find strength to cope with disappointment and heartbreak by trusting in the wisdom and love of God. This is a powerful, moving testimony to the power of faith in the midst of the deepest trials.

Tony Horsfall, retreat leader, author and church leader

Through honest sharing of their experience of living with cancer, and thoughtful reflections on the Christmas story, Isabel and Oliver give eloquent testimony to the radical power of God's presence to bring encouragement, peace, and hope. Whether for those living with cancer themselves, or for those supporting them, this book overflows with authentic, practical & hard-won wisdom which will, I believe, bring blessing and help to many.

Dr David Goudie, Paediatric Consultant, Raigmore Hospital, Inverness

Through Oliver and Isabel's video testimony during the pandemic, many people were greatly helped by the way they shared their raw experience of cancer with faith and hope in God. Now in the pages of this beautifully written book a wider audience can benefit from their story which is interwoven with God's story. The choice of Advent readings encourages us to trust in the God who is with us in times of suffering.

Pastor Alasdair Macleod, Culduthel Christian Centre

Oliver and Isabel's very personal journal of pain, grief and loss is not only sharply observed but is profoundly God-centred and moving. Writing in this joint way, with both personal story and Scripture, highlights so well the power of both human love and God's all-sufficient grace.

Revd Andrew Rollinson, Baptist Minister

Living
with Cancer,
Walking with God

Oliver and Isabel Vellacott

Living
with Cancer,
Walking with God

WAVERLEY ABBEY
RESOURCES

Published 2022 by Waverley Abbey Resources, an operating name of CWR, Waverley Abbey House, Waverley Lane, Farnham, Surrey GU9 8EP, UK. Registered Charity No. 294387. Registered limited company No. 1990308.

For a list of National Distributors, visit waverleyabbeyresources.org/distributors

Concept development and editing by Waverley Abbey Resources.

Design and production by Nord Compo.

Paperback ISBN: 978-1-78951-433-9
eBook ISBN: 978-1-78951-438-4

Dedicated to Isabel's mother, Margaret Seaton

Contents

Introduction

One in two people in the UK will be diagnosed with cancer in their lifetime, which makes this little book directly relevant to 50 percent of its potential readership. And, we believe, still hugely relevant to the other 50 percent!

We are a couple who have been living with cancer for nearly three years. The Stage 4 diagnosis was made just four months into our marriage, which radically changed our perspective on the time we would have together.

We were asked to put together a video testimony describing our experiences, which many who have watched it have said really resonated with them. The thought behind this short book is to similarly connect, but with a much wider audience. It has been written with every kind of reader in mind. You may be on a cancer journey yourself or caring for someone with cancer. You may be a person of faith, but perhaps not. Our intent is simply to try to shine some light, no matter how feeble, on your path.

A transcript of the video testimony is printed verbatim as Appendix 2, and you may wish to read this at some point to help gain a context for these twelve meditations. Everyone looks at life through their own eyes, but each of us can have our perspective enhanced by seeing things through the eyes of others too. With this in mind, in each of the chapters a personal perspective is followed by insights gleaned from the Christmas story. You could read these daily meditations during the twelve days of Christmas, although this book is by no means intended only for the Advent season.

Our title, *Living with Cancer, Walking with God*, is a kind of motto that we adopted early on in our cancer journey. Along with a host of fellow travellers, our story has been complicated by the COVID-19 pandemic, limiting as it has the usual face-to-face contact with friends and family as well as impacting the cancer treatment.

Cancer is truly a terrible disease, but we have been encouraged by these words (which we have had framed on our kitchen window-sill throughout our cancer journey) that there are things that cancer can't do:

It cannot cripple love
It cannot shatter hope
It cannot corrode faith
It cannot eat away peace
It cannot destroy confidence
It cannot kill friendship
It cannot shut out memories
It cannot silence courage
It cannot invade the soul
It cannot reduce eternal life
It cannot quench the Spirit
It cannot lessen the power
    of the resurrection[1]

Every person has a story to tell – and so does God. His is the big story that encompasses our personal stories. He graciously and with ultimate wisdom weaves each of our stories into His story with threads sometimes dark, sometimes bright. The great model for this is the earthly life of Jesus Christ.

You may have never connected cancer with Christmas, but we trust that through these pages you may view both with new eyes.

But before that, let us introduce ourselves.

---

1. Dr Robert L Lynn, https://www.scrapbook.com/poems/doc/4878.html Accessed April 2022

Isabel

Isabel was born the elder of twin girls on North Uist in the Outer Hebrides. Her father died suddenly when she was just six years old. When she was twelve, the family moved to the Scottish mainland where Isabel completed her schooling before training as a nurse in Glasgow. She remained there for twenty years before moving to Inverness. Isabel's expertise in nursing sick and premature babies was developed throughout that time and further developed at Raigmore Hospital, Inverness, over the next nineteen years, where she was appointed as an Advanced Neo-Natal Practitioner, retiring in 2019 upon receiving her cancer diagnosis.

Isabel lived a very healthy lifestyle, enjoying walking, running and cycling. She maintained a huge circle of friends and family and was active in Christian work in church life and beyond. She was famed for her generous hospitality.

Isabel travelled widely internationally, including to Uganda to work at Wakisa Pregnancy Centre for young girls in Kampala.

Isabel was just fifty-nine years old when she died.

(A much fuller description of Isabel's life, taken from the Thanksgiving Service for her life, is reproduced in Appendix 1.)

Oliver

Following his graduation, Oliver taught Mathematics to graduate level for several years while also pursuing postgraduate studies in computer science before moving into the nascent but fast-developing world of network-based interactive computing. He was involved in the introduction of the first commercially available such system in Europe in the mid-1960s.

This led to an increasing interest in the development of software tools for end-users seeking to build their own applications, and to this end he joined together with a colleague in a business that followed this goal with considerable success worldwide.

Through a vivid vision of Jesus in his late teens, which has lived with Oliver ever since, came a sense of calling into some kind of Christian ministry. This sense reached maturity in the late 1970s, and he gradually stepped back from business life and moved toward pastoral leadership in church. His particular calling was into pioneering new churches, the first of these being in Wiltshire, England back in 1980. He has always wanted to encourage this kind of 'spiritual entrepreneurship' and to support pastors involved in such enterprises. To this end he established a couple of charitable trusts. He also ran a retreat centre for those in ministry for twenty years. He retired from active pastoral leadership of a church (a final 'church plant') in 2017.

Oliver was married in his early twenties to Valerie, a nurse at Guy's Hospital, and they had six children. Valerie, his wife of fifty-two years, suffered from Alzheimer's disease latterly and tragically died quite suddenly. Since then, Oliver remarried – to Isabel – and embarked on a whole new journey, some of which is described in this book. Both of these marriages, though very different, were remarkable in many ways.

Today, Oliver has fifteen grandchildren and six great-grandchildren.

CHAPTER 1

Shock

Isabel

We had been married for only a few months when a quick appointment at the hospital indicated all was not well. I was being referred to the urgent cancer list the following week so had to cancel our planned holiday to the Isle of Skye. This was the beginning of our cancer journey – or adventure, as we sometimes like to call it.

After working in the NHS for forty years, I had a lot of knowledge about what this might mean, but the reality did not sink in easily. We did share this information with some close friends, including our pastor and his wife. These very close friends (my 'inner circle' as I like to call them) and our church family would be the backbone in our lives as we started to navigate CT scans, MRI scans and surgeries.

One of my memories from that time was the feeling that I was letting people down. It's a strange thing to think, but throughout my working days my plan was that when semi- or fully- retired I would be able to help my mum – much like she had done for us following her early widowhood.

When the actual confirmation of how extensive the cancer was (Stage 4, having spread in many places) came, the tears didn't actually flow. We were in a state of shock. Maybe it was my way of processing the news initially – I don't know – but very soon when meeting up with family and seeing their tears, ours flowed and flowed. But "weeping may endure for a night, but a shout of joy comes in the morning" (Psalm 30:5, Amplified).

I was due to retire officially just six days after the diagnosis. So, under-
standably, my colleagues were very shocked to hear the news too.

Oliver and I had many questions swimming around in our heads:

1. Our future was changing. Following retiral, we had plans of trips
we wanted to do. I had been keen to go back to Africa to assist in a project
I had visited twice before, but this would now be unlikely. What would
our future look like now?

2. Would I even be given treatment, or would I be sent to the hospice?
This was a very real thought in those initial days, although surgery to
prevent obstruction plus chemotherapy were offered.

3. Would our new marriage survive these very challenging circumstances?

4. I didn't want pity but did want others to know of the faith I had.
But, when the rubber hit the road, how would my faith stand up to this
new challenge?

Oliver

There were not just one but two miraculous births at the first Christmas,
and both came as a huge shock – Zechariah and Elizabeth became parents
at an advanced age, and Mary and Joseph had had no sexual intercourse
during their betrothal. So, what was going on? The answer is that God was
'going on', doing something very significant in both cases.

His plans were gradually revealed to them, but the initial shock
showed: Zechariah did not even believe it (Luke 1:18), and Mary (who
was 'greatly troubled') responded by saying, 'How will this be… since I am
a virgin?' (Luke 1:34). Joseph was so shocked that he intended to divorce
Mary (Matthew 1:19).

In each instance, though, there was an intervention from God – a message delivered by an angel – assuring each that something else was 'going
on'. Mary realised this and broke into a praise song to God (Luke 1:46–55),
as did Zechariah (Luke 1:68–79). Joseph, who was really struggling, had
his mind put at rest by the visiting angel's words and was even granted the
privilege of giving Mary's child his name: Jesus (Matthew 1:19).

And so, it was Jesus who was revealed through the shocks each of them
experienced. Indeed, Zechariah and Elizabeth's son (John the Baptist)

was the herald of Jesus, declaring, 'He is the one who comes after me, the straps of whose sandals I am not worthy to untie' (John 1:27).

It is our prayer, dear reader, that in the midst of your own times of shock, you become aware of a divine hand at work in your life.

CHAPTER 2

Timing

Isabel

Having been diagnosed and retired at the time of my diagnosis, a farewell event was not high in my list of priorities. After a couple of attempts, it was finally arranged for a date in early March (2020). This date did not seem too significant at the time, although we did know that COVID-19 was sweeping through China and would probably also spread through Europe into the UK.

As I look back on that very happy occasion with colleagues, I can see God's hand in it all. If we hadn't met together then, one year on and still in lockdown, we would still not be able to meet together. For me and my many work friends, it was a special day when I was able to share what God was doing in my life and could also tell them about the book *Beyond the Big C* [1]. I'm forever grateful to have had that opportunity – at just the right time.

As we had only been married for four months, many felt sorry for us. However, my twin sister had, on the day of my diagnosis, commented that our marriage was 'for such a time as this' – a reference to the story of Esther in the Bible (see Esther 4:14). We then realised that God's impeccable timing of my diagnosis was exactly at the right time for us in our marriage, and for our family and friends.

Looking back, we can see God's perfect timing in so many aspects of our lives in the days and weeks since that diagnosis.

---

1. Jeremy Marshall, *Beyond the Big C* (Leyland, England: 10Publishing, 2019).

Oliver

For the Christian believer, life is not haphazard. And nor were the events of the Christmas story. Consider for a moment the astronomical event that coincided with the birth of Jesus. The astrologers, or scholars, from the East who visited Jesus had studied the heavens and noted a significant sign in the skies (Matthew 2:1). This was God's timing.

We are also told that what the angel Gabriel spoke to Zechariah about the birth of John, the forerunner of Jesus, indicated "my words will be fulfilled at their proper time" (Luke 1:20, Amplified). We are also told about Mary's unique role in Jesus' birth, "When the set time had fully come, God sent his Son, born of a woman" (Galatians 4:4).

Very often appearances seem to contradict this message of God's perfect timing. The very writing of the four accounts of the life of Jesus (found in the Gospels) appears to lack anyone in charge until we realise that God's Holy Spirit was actually superintending what was being written down. Scripture, from Genesis to Revelation, is not haphazard but tells the overarching story of God's dealings with humankind – and notably, His own entry into the human scene there in Bethlehem, as promised and at just the right time.

One of the things we increasingly learn is that our time is rarely the same as His time. This is why we are encouraged to wait for His time in the working out of our lives, knowing that, as this paraphrase of Scripture puts it, 'Waiting does not diminish us, any more than waiting diminishes a pregnant mother. We are enlarged in the waiting. We, of course, don't see what is enlarging us. But the longer we wait, the larger we become, and the more joyful our expectancy' (Romans 8:22–25, *The Message*).

It's all to do with entrusting our lives into God's hands, knowing that His thoughts and plans are so much greater than ours can ever be. This extract from the poem *My Times Are in Thy Hand* by W.F. Lloyd expresses it beautifully:

My times are in thy hand;
my God, I wish them there;
my life, my friends, my soul, I leave
entirely to thy care.

My times are in thy hand,
whatever they may be;
pleasing or painful, dark or bright,
as best may seem to thee.

W.F. Lloyd (1824)[2]

---

2. Lyrics sourced from hymnary.org/text/my_times_are_in_thy_hand_my_god_i_wish Accessed April 2022

CHAPTER 3

Anger and Guilt

Isabel

When you have been given a terminal diagnosis there is such a mix of emotions, and anger and guilt are often felt keenly.

For myself, anger was not an initial emotion in my cancer journey. My life may have been too busy in the weeks following diagnosis, with two surgeries and chemotherapy-planning appointments. It was not until the first morning after my first chemo cycle, approximately four weeks after surgery, that I experienced anger.

I woke up crying, feeling awful and angry, although I couldn't actually pinpoint whom I was angry with. Many people might be angry with God, but for me this was not the case. My first thoughts went to an incident described early on in the Bible. How did Joseph feel in the bottom of the pit his brothers had thrown him into? (Genesis 37). That day I felt it was me at the bottom of that pit. I felt so far from God.

In the midst of the anger that morning we were able to cry out to God in prayer, quite literally letting the tears flow. That awful feeling of being so distant from God was very strong and very frightening too. I've had few other episodes of feeling so angry, but I've realised it can be difficult to differentiate between anger and heavy sadness.

Having worked in the NHS for nearly forty years and in the neo-natal unit as an Advanced Neo-Natal Nurse Practitioner, I have seen and experienced much anger and sadness when breaking bad news. Nowadays there are courses on how to break bad news to people, but actually bad news is bad news and cannot be sugared-coated in any way. But there are ways to be more sensitive, and I have seen the way we have delivered devastating news change over the years.

You will always remember the way sad news is broken to you. My dad died when my twin sister and I were six years of age, and my brother was three. I can still remember much about the conversations that took place before we were actually told that he had died. But the memories around that occasion are of kindness and compassion, and again I feel no anger about his death, but I do feel very, very sad. To this day it's the saddest news I've ever had to hear – sadder than my own cancer diagnosis.

I always prided myself in having a healthy lifestyle – running and cycling and eating well. But seeing people who had clearly abused their bodies with too much food, drink, and nicotine got to me. I had to pull my emotions in and realise that I was not to be the judge of other people, no matter what I thought about their lifestyle. Having said this, I was quite proud always of my lunch box, which resembled a greengrocer's store!

As mentioned earlier, I was on a phased retirement with one week of work left but felt cheated and angry when I was diagnosed just at that point. Having worked in the NHS for forty years, it wasn't the way I had planned to retire. I felt the rug had been ripped from under my feet. I had gone from being a nurse practitioner to being a patient overnight, with no time to prepare for the transition.

I have a wide circle of close friends and family, but while I shared the news of my diagnosis when appropriate, I found comments and questioning quite threatening and felt I had to protect both myself and my family. People sometimes don't know what to say, but rather than face silence, they say something inappropriate. It may be that they've had little experience of such situations and are just trying to be kind, although sadly it comes across the wrong way.

Oliver

If ever there were such a mixture of anger and guilt, surely it was in the heart of Joseph when he first became aware of Mary's pregnancy. Anger at her apparent unfaithfulness and guilt vicariously for Mary who had surely brought shame on them both.

Like any young couple, they had plans. These were now scuppered, or at least drastically changed. Suddenly, out of nowhere, Joseph was now saddled with a future he hadn't asked for.

Of course, once the angel had visited him and explained what was going on, the complexion of the situation changed (Matthew 1:18–21). The feelings of guilt had been unfounded. For us, very often our sense of guilt can be baseless too. It can even be totally in our imagination, as in the familiar 'guilt trip'. Reality kicked in for Joseph when his life was touched by heaven. Even so, he was likely bewildered by what all of this would mean for him and his young family.

What went through Joseph's mind on that arduous journey from Nazareth to Bethlehem (Luke 2)? He was now responsible for a pregnant wife and a baby that wasn't his! Yet he did know that God was at work, difficult and challenging though his life had now become.

For myself, anger and guilt have often gone together. This happened often in church leadership when hearing of something happening within the church family, being initially angry and then discovering that I had only heard half the truth, whereupon there was guilt for reacting with anger to it.

In our cancer journey I can honestly say that I have not been angry with God, even though the cancer invaded our life so soon after our wedding. I am struck by the words of Job, a man who lost everything including his health. He was told (by his wife!) to 'curse God and die', but he responded, 'Shall we accept good from God, and not trouble?' (Job 2:9–10).[1] However, I do feel guilt at times that I am not being a sufficiently good caregiver. Emotions are complex enough in any marriage, but when complicated by terminal illness they can become quite tricky. All I can do is look to God for sufficient grace and to remember that there is a bigger picture behind it all, as there was for Job... and Joseph.

One can't help but feel for Joseph, managing as he was such a complex set of emotions. But he did accept God's will, settled down, was a good

---

1. For a comprehensive and incisive treatment of Job's suffering, I recommend Mike Mason, *The Gospel According to Job* (Wheaton, Illinois: Crossway Books, 1994).

and loving father, taught his son his trade, etc. The fact that Jesus was obedient to both his parents points to this. Just as Moses was 'faithful in all God's house' (Hebrews 3:2) so Joseph was faithful in his own household, nurturing no less a person than God's Son. He is a model for us when we are potentially consumed by anger and guilt.

Both Moses and Joseph were quite simply close to the heart of God.

O Jesus, blest Redeemer,
Sent from the heart of God,
Hold us, who wait before Thee,
Near to the heart of God.

Cleland Boyd McAfee (1866-1944)[2]

---

2. *Near to the heart of God*, sourced from www.hymnal.net/en/hymn/h/375 Accessed April 2022

CHAPTER 4

Pain

Isabel

Pain can manifest itself in so many different ways and differently in every one of us.

The physical pain I suffer is not hugely problematic… The pain that truly hurts is the pain I feel in my heart where no one can see it, no one can hear it, and no one notices me wince. The pain I felt in those early days was such that I imagined my heart would break into many tiny little pieces, as I saw the effect this illness was having on my nearest and dearest.

I saw them trying to second guess how I was feeling – then I would catch their eyes full of tears but still trying to be strong for me. I can still feel that deep pain even just thinking about it two years on.

A few months after diagnosis my surgeons thought I might be eligible for surgery in Glasgow to remove part of my liver, which contained tumours. We had two long consultations in Glasgow with the surgeons there explaining the length of the surgery and the after-effects. A second stoma was a possibility to collect my urine, in addition to my existing ileostomy. We knew it would be a long process, involving intensive care and a long recovery time. All the while, there would be the potential that my cancer would spread more.

Seven months after diagnosis, and following another CT scan, more cancer spread was detected, which meant that surgery was no longer a possibility, and never would be.

The pain on hearing this news was awful again for us but also for our family and friends who had been so delighted for us prior to this.

Looking back, I know all these details were in God's hands. I would have found the time in Glasgow away from family and friends difficult and can see His leading in these very painful days. Sometimes we can only see this when we look back.

Oliver

Pain figures in the Christmas story through the actions of King Herod. As a result of his actions, the pain of grief looms large in 'The Slaughter of the Innocents', the murder of all baby boys in Bethlehem two years old and younger (Matthew 2:13-18). In the providence of God, Joseph and Mary had escaped experiencing the slaughter of their own child, but, in reality, their own grief was merely put 'on hold'. Jesus would be slaughtered thirty years later, and Mary would witness this horrific act first-hand at the foot of the cross. When the baby Jesus was presented in the Temple, an old man, Simeon, had prophesied this: 'This child is destined to cause the falling and rising of many in Israel, and to be a sign that will be spoken against, so that the thoughts of many hearts will be revealed. And a sword will pierce your own soul too' (Luke 2:34–35).

As we can see, Christmas is not just a pleasant story of a baby in a manger, as it can be misrepresented as being. All human pain is bound up in this story! Jesus knows what life is like; He knows what pain is; He knows grief big-time (Lamentations 1:12). He was even described as 'a man of suffering, and familiar with pain' (Isaiah 53:3). His story draws me in and gives meaning and substance to my own pain. The hero of this story (Immanuel, 'God with us') identifies with me and, in the process, actually saves me (Hebrews 2:14–15) and promises me a future beyond my imagining.

So, how do I live with pain, whether it is brought about by living with a terminal illness or possibly by separation from some of one's own children, as has been the case with me since I remarried as a widower? Well, I simply rest in God's future. I know that as a child of God, pain and suffering will one day give way to glory (Romans 8:17).

His purposes will ripen fast,
Unfolding ev'ry hour;
The bud may have a bitter taste,
But sweet will be the flow'r.

(William Cowper 1774)[1]

---

1. *God Moves in a Mysterious Way*, sourced from hymnary.org/text/god_moves_in_a
_mysterious_way Accessed April 2022

CHAPTER 5

Song

Isabel

'He took me from a fearful pit' (Psalm 40:2). I sang this verse from Psalm 40 frequently growing up and memorised the whole chapter too! The pit being referred to was similar to a pit I saw when we visited Masada in Israel on a trip there a few years back. I always assumed a pit was full of soil, but this deep pit was made from massive boulders, making it very difficult to scramble out of. So, when I sing this psalm now, I am aware of the difficulties of escaping from it.

When I went into hospital for my first surgery, I made up a playlist on my phone with a selection of songs, which were all a real and true blessing. When I was too tired to read, I was able to listen to this music.

Having songs that have helped me during my illness has also enabled me to share such with others going through trials – and I am so thankful for these opportunities.

Lou Fellingham's song *Everlasting Arms (Lean Hard)* had a huge impact. The lyrics spoke to me again and again:

He lavishes grace as our burdens grow greater
He sends us more strength as our labours increase
To added afflictions He offers more mercy
To multiplied trials He multiplies peace

When we have exhausted our store of endurance
When our strength has failed and the day is half done
When we've reached the end of our earthly resources

Our Father's full giving is only begun
Our Father's full giving is only begun

> So lean hard
> Lean hard
> Lean on the everlasting arms
> Lean hard
> Lean hard
> Lean on the everlasting arms
> Lean on the everlasting arms[1]

Oliver

There are three songs that form part of the Christmas story – sung by the angels to the shepherds, by Mary as an expectant mother, and by Zechariah at the birth of John the Baptist (see Luke 2:14; 1:46–55, 68–79).

Clearly then, there is something about giving expression to what's going on within and around us in song that is part instinctive and part cathartic and, for people of faith, part worship.

How I would have loved to hear that angels' song! I am sure it would have been an incredible sight, as they are described as 'a great company of the heavenly host' (Luke 2:13). I hope they will repeat that performance (just for me!) in heaven. Their song was of worship: 'Glory to God in the highest heaven'. But we earthly creatures have even greater reason than they to glorify God because of the second half of their hymn: 'on earth peace to those upon whom His favour rests'. To know this favour is to be raised way above our earth-bound status to be seated 'in the heavenly realms' (Ephesians 2:6). Zechariah had been struck dumb for the nine months of Elizabeth's pregnancy, but following the naming of the child his tongue was freed directly into song (Luke 2: 68-79). How cathartic that must have been! He began with worship before addressing the role of his baby boy to 'go on before the Lord to prepare the way for him' (Luke 1:76). This was a salvation song. John was 'to give his people the knowledge of salvation through the forgiveness of their sins' (Luke 1:77).

---

1. Lou Fellingham, *Everlasting Arms Lean Hard*, Thank You Music Ltd, 2016

Possessing assurance of this salvation makes the world of difference when going through any kind of trial; we always have a sure and steadfast hope anchored in God's mercy.

Mary's song, known as the 'Magnificat', truly is magnificent (Luke 1:46–55). It contrasts our humble state with God ('the Mighty One') in His mercy toward us – toward me, even little me. 'He has been mindful of the humble state of his servant' (v. 48). She was also given insight beyond her own life, setting her story within God's greater story. There is something that stirs my heart deeply about some of the great oratorios, and especially the choral sections, and even more especially those that are full of worship to God my Saviour. Such music may not be to everyone's taste, but I encourage you to find what speaks into your soul – what is instinctive for you, cathartic and worshipful. There is great balm for the soul to be found in music, such as Isabel discovered with her playlist when facing surgery.

There was one particular song that spoke to both of us in the weeks immediately following diagnosis, and we sometimes sang it together at the piano:

When I fear my faith will fail, Christ will hold me fast;
When the tempter would prevail, He will hold me fast.
I could never keep my hold through life's fearful path;
For my love is often cold; He must hold me fast.

He will hold me fast, He will hold me fast;
For my Saviour loves me so, He will hold me fast.

Those He saves are His delight, Christ will hold me fast;
Precious in His holy sight, He will hold me fast.
He'll not let my soul be lost; His promises shall last;
Bought by Him at such a cost, He will hold me fast.

He will hold me fast, He will hold me fast;
For my Saviour loves me so, He will hold me fast.

For my life He bled and died, Christ will hold me fast;
Justice has been satisfied; He will hold me fast.

Raised with Him to endless life, He will hold me fast
Till our faith is turned to sight, when He comes at last.

He will hold me fast, He will hold me fast;
For my Saviour loves me so, He will hold me fast.

(Ada Ruth Habershon / Matt Merker)[2]

---

2. *When I Fear My Faith Will Fail (He Will Hold Me Fast)*, 2013 Getty Music Publishing (BMI) / Matthew Merker Music (BMI).

CHAPTER 6

Uncertainty and God's Will

Isabel

In this world, nothing is certain. Yes, we can make plans and hope the dates align with those plans, but no matter how much planning, our time of entering this world to when we leave is outside our control, no matter how much knowledge is involved at both ends of the spectrum.

I have worked in neo-natal units most of my life and have watched as parents have planned for the delivery of their babies, but the reality has often been very different from their plans. What does the future hold then? Yes, it's important to make *some* plans, being careful to have food in the home (not excessive though) and also money for a rainy day (again, not excessive), but in the Bible Jesus reminds us: 'Look at the birds of the air; they do not sow or reap or store away in barns, and yet your heavenly Father feeds them. Are you not much more valuable than they? Can any one of you by worrying add a single hour to your life? And why do you worry about clothes?... But seek first his kingdom and his righteousness, and all these things will be given to you as well' (Matthew 6:26–28,33).

In February 2020, COVID came pretty much out of the blue, but it has afforded the opportunity for many of us, with or without cancer, to refocus our lives and really assess what is important and what is not.

For me there is something very exciting about remaining fully dependent on God. When we live in the centre of God's will, we have meaning and purpose in our lives instead of aimlessly wavering from this to that. As a child, Corrie ten Boom knew intense danger, as her family hid Jews in their home during the Second World War, and she endured time in a concentration camp. And yet she could still write: 'Never be afraid to trust an unknown future to a known God.'[1]

During my adventure I have experienced some pitying voices – and looks too. People have made comments such as: 'Oh, it's a pity you're just married', 'What a pity you're just retired', or 'It's a pity you won't be able to travel'. Such people do not see what we see – that we are centred in God's will. Those to be really pitied are those with no resurrection hope. As it says in the Bible, 'If only for this life we have hope in Christ, we are of all people most to be pitied' (1 Corinthians 15:19).

Oliver

When thinking about or facing suffering, I am drawn to one particular section of the Bible – the book of Job. Groping desperately for some help in the midst of extreme suffering, Job longed for one thing (or, rather, one person) – a mediator between himself and God (see Job 9:33–35). This is stated amid much uncertainty in chapter nine but issues into the most confident of assertions in a later chapter:

I know that my redeemer lives,
and that in the end he will stand on the earth.
And after my skin has been destroyed,
yet in my flesh I will see God;
I myself will see him
with my own eyes – I, and not another.
How my heart yearns within me! (Job 19: 25–27)

We can be even more certain of this one fact – there *is* a mediator! He came to us that first Christmas. His name? Immanuel – God with us (Matthew 1:23). Mary and Joseph were also told by the angel to call him Jesus. Why? 'Because he will save his people from their sins' (Matthew 1:21).

---

1. Corrie Ten Boom, quoted in www.goodreads.com/author/quotes/102203.Corrie_ten_Boom

This is quite simply the greatest news humanity has ever heard. Clearly, despite their many questions and facing huge uncertainties, Mary and Joseph were in the very centre of God's will. And when the shepherds and the wise men visited, they confirmed it with their worship and their very significant gifts (see Matthew 2:11) – gold for a King (indicating He is our LORD), frankincense for a Great High Priest (our Mediator), and myrrh for His sacrificial death (our Saviour).

It was God's will that Jesus should suffer, but the outcome is all-glorious and all-certain (see Romans 8:18). We, too, can go through suffering and be in the very centre of God's will throughout, knowing that the outcome, for us as for Him, will be glorious. We have a hope, which this song by Stuart Townend and Mark Edwards reflects on:[2]

There is a hope that lifts my weary head,
A consolation strong against despair,
That when the world has plunged me in its deepest pit,
I find the Saviour there!
Through present sufferings, future's fear,
He whispers 'courage' in my ear.
For I am safe in everlasting arms,
And they will lead me home.

2. *There is a Hope*, Stuart Townend & Mark Edwards, 2007, Thankyou Music

CHAPTER 7

Focus

Isabel

As I've written, my diagnosis came when I was entering another chapter in my life. I'd worked full time till retirement and had tried to help out at church and with Alpha courses as well as cooking at church camps, travelling to Africa to help with a Christian project. I was looking forward in retirement to focusing on these things 100 percent.

I always loved entertaining, whether it was simple suppers on a weeknight or cooking a roast for Sunday lunch. This included catering for Christianity Explored or Alpha course groups. I'd been involved in leading some classes, but some folks (who are now dear friends) felt they would rather repeat the course in smaller groups, so myself and a lovely friend from church would meet at my house on a weekday evening, sit round the table and go over the course again, which really helped these women. It was just two of us and two of them, and it really helped us all discuss in our small group what we might not feel able to discuss in a larger group.

So, I'm a firm believer in mentoring-type courses for people who have attended classes to help their faith grow. It also helps them to see what life is like as a Christian, to see the ups and downs and that a lot of the time it's not plain sailing. Most weeks we all had prayer requests, whether we were twenty or eighty years of age, and however long we had been a Christian.

Shortly after we married, Oliver and I were approached by friends of mine to see if we would be interested in using our home for a day retreat for couples. My friends were both counsellors, and we and they felt we had the space to be able to provide this. We prayed that this would be the right avenue to explore, and a date was picked in June 2019. This was a lot of my desires and loves coming together – entertaining, sharing God's Word and getting close to people. But four months prior to this event we were dealt the blow that I had Stage 4 cancer, and we would be unable to pursue this. I wondered then if we had prayed enough and listened enough to God. I was also concerned about the many doubts we were having.

We then realised that the path was changing. Focusing on Jesus would still continue, albeit not in the way we had envisaged. Again, 'living with cancer, walking with God' became an even stronger motto for us.

Like Job in the Old Testament, we want to know the whys, hows, and wherefores, as if putting it into a logical framework would ease our suffering! The book of Job does reveal that the reasoning that bad things happen to good people may have a much broader context than we imagine. We simply cannot understand the working of an almighty, sovereign God by rational thinking alone. We must leave room for faith in the mercy, goodness, and justice of a God who loves us with an incomprehensible passion.

Oliver

Just as our eyes shift focus when something new comes into our field of vision, likewise our hearts when circumstances change in life. For sure, our focus since Isabel's diagnosis radically shifted. I would like to be able to say it shifted from being earth-bound to being heavenward-bound, or at least to living between heaven and earth. It certainly intensified our focus on what God had to say to us in the moment. We prayed together, often in tears, in a way that cast ourselves on God like never before, remembering His promises never to abandon us and to give us strength (one of my favourite verses), 'as your days, so shall your strength be' (Deuteronomy 33:25, ESV).[1]

---

1. Every evening when we prayed together, we found two resources very helpful: Sarah Young, *Jesus Always* (Nashville, Tennessee: Thomas Nelson, 2016) and the *Lectio 365* app, which is available to download from Apple or the Google Play Store.

For Joseph and Mary, the shift of focus was dramatic when they were told what was to come. As a matter of interest, how well would *you* be able to focus on an angel speaking to you?

The Old Testament prophecies of Jesus' coming also involved a sudden shift of focus on the prophets' part (see for example, Isaiah 9:6–7), as if the sun had suddenly burst through the clouds for a moment.

A lot of things were taken away from Mary and Joseph as they received their startling revelation of what their future life would look like. Theirs would no longer be a 'normal', comfortable, unremarkable life. For a start, they didn't even have a decent cot into which to lay the newborn baby. Their very lives were in danger too (from Herod's murderous troops), and they became refugees in a foreign land (Egypt); much further pain lay in store for them.

There is always a 'but' in Scripture, and the but in their story is that God directed it to be instrumental in working out the greatest story ever told — God's saving plan for humanity.

As for our story, our marriage has not been as we imagined. We thought we would be walking together the rest of our days and then within four months got the news that we would also be walking with terminal cancer. Two years on, our marriage was described by a close friend as 'a great love story'. It is humbling and touching to hear this, but we are even more deeply touched and humbled by the great love story of which we are part. Isabel has already referred to God's incomprehensible passion. This is the love of Jesus for my soul. As the hymn *Jesus the Very Thought of Thee* puts it:

> But what to those who find? Ah, this
> Nor tongue nor pen can show;
> The love of Jesus, what it is
> None but His loved ones know.

Bernard of Clairvaux (1090-1153)[2]

---

2. Sourced from www.hymnal.net/en/hymn/h/209

God bankrupted heaven when Jesus (who is God Himself) came and paid an infinite price on my behalf. Why? We encourage you to answer the question for yourself (Ephesians 3:16–19 is a helpful place to start).

CHAPTER 8

Relationship

Isabel

As a Christian, my life is centered around relationships. As Christians we surely take the needs of others that bit more seriously. Relationships are central to the stories found in the Bible – for example, between Jesus and His disciples. Of course, some relationships are more significant than others, and the loss of my dad when I was only six years old naturally has had a huge effect on my own outlook on life.

My mum was never bitter or angry with God about the sudden death of our dad at such a young age, and this communicated to myself and my siblings a healthy understanding of death. In this time of my illness, that understanding has remained influential in the way we deal with and discuss the prospect of dying.

To have Mum's perspective was something that carried us through the deeper, darker days. We are so thankful to have had a believing and godly mother.

Getting married just four months before my diagnosis brought additional stability to my life. Many people were saying how sorry they felt for us, but for me to have a soulmate was a huge blessing. We knew it would be a difficult road; I had seen others facing difficulties that brought about disintegration, but for us this trouble brought the two of us much closer. We faced this journey together, which has been described by one of my consultants as 'not a sprint but a marathon'.

My close friends also made a commitment for this marathon journey, which proved the depth of their friendship in a beautiful way. We were not only supported by people in this country but also by others in countries across the globe. To hear my name spoken in a recording sent to us of a prayer meeting in a language I did not understand meant a lot to me. It made me realise that my God is also at work through the whole worldwide family of believers, my brothers and sisters.

I said on the day of my diagnosis that I wanted my life to be a witness to whomever I met, whether people in the church, medical personnel, neighbours, friends or family, so that they could see my strength coming from the Lord. Since then, people who are facing similar situations have been in contact with me, and I have been able to give them a helpful perspective on what cancer is like. While every cancer is different, I hope I have been able to give them useful pointers. It has been interesting how many have been happy to connect with me for this reason.

Besides all this, we have often received unprompted messages from friends who were unaware of anything specific happening on a particular day. This is always encouraging – to know that God has gone ahead of us. Sometimes in this country we are hesitant about listening to God when He is prompting us to act or to say an encouraging word to another person, but God Himself encourages us to take every opportunity to 'fan into flame the gift of God' (2 Timothy 1:6).

Oliver

The COVID lockdown of 2020/21 showed the importance of relationship to us all. Living in isolation proved to be responsible for a further mental health 'pandemic'.

God lives in relationship (Father, Son, Holy Spirit), and by making us 'in his own image' (Genesis 1:27) we are relational beings too. What 'makes us tick' are our relationships, whether family, friends, or work colleagues. So, it is no surprise that Jesus was born into a family unit and grew up in a normal family home with siblings, around his adoptive father Joseph's carpentry business, with the daily chat on the street in Nazareth.

Jesus also has an ancestry of relationships. In writing of His birth, two of the Gospel writers (Matthew and Luke) are at pains to point this out and to list all the generational relationships. In Luke's case this goes all the way back to Adam, the first human being and created by God. Adam is described in this list as 'son of God' (Luke 3:38) for this reason.

Why are all these names so painstakingly listed? Surely because Jesus is inextricably connected into the stuff of our human life from His very birth. Some of the names in his genealogy are most surprising. There's Judah (who committed incest), Rahab (a prostitute), and Bathsheba (an adulterous relationship). And as if to make the point that Jesus, though born a Jew, did not come solely for the Jews, also included is Ruth, a Gentile (Matthew 1:1–17). Jesus was without sin, but identified Himself with our sinful human plight, as He still does.

The ultimate relationship any of us can ever have is with God. (In fact, if only we knew it, this is the reason we were made.) Jesus came to bring us back to God. He is the vital link between our humanity and our creator. In short, He reconciles us to God (see Ephesians 2:14–22).

The Christmas story in itself is a fascinating mix of relationships: Joseph, Mary and the babe, cousin Elizabeth, the shepherds, the Magi, Herod, Simeon, Anna – and the angels, who announced this higher, deeper, more profound relationship for those 'on whom his favour rests' (Luke 2:14).

We believe it is this relationship into which Jesus has brought both Isabel and myself that sweetens and energises our own relationship as husband and wife and every other relationship we enjoy. And all these relationships have been made all the more intense and meaningful amid the ravages of cancer.

Relationships can come and go but some endure over the years for both of us. Our relationship with God endures forever, and, among many other things, this means that if this is our last day on earth then it is our first day in heaven!

You may like to make this prayer your own: 'Lord Jesus, I thank you for making a relationship with me and for sticking closer than a brother. In all my relationships with others may I clothe myself in compassion, kindness, humility, gentleness, and patience. Help me to humbly and freely forgive others as you have forgiven me.'

CHAPTER 9

Prayer

Isabel

This is possibly the most important chapter in this book, but the hardest to put down on paper.

Following the diagnosis two and a half years ago, our minds were taken over by the question of whether I was going to survive for any time at all. This made putting aside time to speak to God quite difficult. But despite all of this we knew, even at the early stage of our cancer journey, that we were being prayed for, even when we felt it was so hard for us to communicate in prayer ourselves.

I had to mentally hand everything over to God and let Him control the illness with the help of the medical team. While it can be all too tempting to try to control things, we knew that God was our ultimate help.

We have had numerous examples of answers to prayer where the person praying for us had no idea what was needed or required but had been prompted by God to pray for a specific need.

The people praying for us throughout the world are continuing to pray more than two years on from diagnosis, many praying daily – an example of praying without ceasing (see 1 Thessalonians 5:17, ESV). There is nothing like waking up in the morning to find a text message or prayer already waiting to encourage us for that day.

We have also had a special evening of prayer with the elders of our church, which included anointing me with oil as encouraged in scripture (James 5:14).

Praying together as husband and wife has been raised to a whole new level due to the sudden cessation of my previous busy lifestyle, giving us more time for each other and for contemplation. Every time we had a hospital appointment (at least fortnightly, sometimes more often) we would park the car in the hospital car park in exactly the same place and pray together for the upcoming treatment. This place has become our place of prayer, our 'holy ground'. One of the things we prayed for specifically on these occasions was that I would have contact with a Christian during my time in hospital. This prayer was answered on most occasions and was a sign to me that God was hearing and answering our prayers. One example was when I was very poorly with renal failure and required renal dialysis overnight. The consultant and the renal nurse were both Christians. In fact, the nurse asked me outright if I was a Christian because there was such a sense of peace in the room.

From the very beginning we prayed that God would work a miracle, but we were aware that He could do so in a number of different ways. The nature of the miracle we left up to Him. It is a miracle that I am still alive so long after a Stage 4 diagnosis and that I have coped well with my treatment.

Prayer changes things and we have proved that!

Oliver

The first Christmas was a time when heaven broke through to earth – the star of Bethlehem breaking through the cosmos, the angels breaking through the sky, the baby Jesus breaking through eternity into time and through Spirit into flesh and blood.

Prayer is surely a kind of 'breaking through' between us and God, between our mortal existence and His eternity, between our flesh-and-blood-lives and His was-and-is-and-is-to-come-life. There are a number of actual prayers in the Advent narrative – Mary's Magnificat, Zechariah's song, and Simeon's song (Luke 2:29–32) being the primary examples. But there are also 'conversational prayers' between individuals and God, often through an angel. Both are aspects of prayer – some more formal, some less so.

What may we learn here?

John the Baptist, the forerunner to Jesus, was an answer to prayer (see Luke 1:13). Zechariah, his father, despite uttering the prayer, couldn't believe it would be answered (just like us!) and had to learn a hard lesson in the process (being struck dumb for more than nine months, as we have seen).

Mary the mother of Jesus, on the other hand, hadn't prayed specifically for a child (certainly not out of wedlock) yet she was to have a baby now anyway. This revelation (from an angel) nonetheless led her to pray.

We have experienced these two kinds of praying – one asking for a miracle and the other reacting in prayer to circumstances thrust upon us that we were not anticipating. Cancer came unbeckoned, but it in turn beckoned prayerfulness in us.

Our own helplessness is good reason to pray. As C.S. Lewis wrote, 'We must lay before God what is in us, not what ought to be in us.' And further, Lewis insightfully wrote: 'The disquieting thing is not that we skimp and begrudge the duty of prayer. The really disquieting thing is it should have to be numbered among duties at all.'[1]

---

1. C.S. Lewis, *Letters to Malcolm: Chiefly on Prayer* (London: William Collins, 2020) pp.27 and 152.

CHAPTER 10

Sharing

Isabel

Everyone has a different approach to how they share news with friends and family. This can prove tricky when it comes to bad news and being a Christian does not minimise the need for sharing. Having many friends, I have to distinguish what news is important to be shared and to be prayed about. I've found this quite hard. People want to be helpful, but sometimes such shared news can grow arms and legs! I was very concerned, for example, about my mum hearing such news secondhand and getting the wrong end of the stick or of her becoming over-anxious about me.

But I knew I had to share how I was feeling and what God was doing in my life and the lives I was in contact with. I also felt it a duty to God to be honest about my feelings and certainly not to appear flippant. Sometimes I likened myself to the psalmist David who was utterly honest before God, calling out in distress and even anger at times. To discover such raw honesty in the Scriptures has been a great encouragement to me.

Some people describe me as being brave, but I was simply doing what anyone would who wanted to prolong their life. However, I did also know that God was in control. I may well have come across as brave, but I have to admit that behind the scenes it was sometimes a different story.

Sharing was certainly not done either to gain sympathy or to put myself centre-stage. I now know that everyone is carrying a burden, whether we see it or not. As the illness has gone on, I have changed the way I share, and I have seen changes reflected in those I've shared with.

What we are doing in this little book is all part of our sharing, but we recognise that in this format it does have its limitations.

Oliver

There was a lot of sharing going on that first Advent, whether angels bringing news from heaven or cousins Mary and Elizabeth chatting over family news. Both Mary and Elizabeth were going to have their first baby, so there would have been no shortage of excited conversation when Mary made the journey down south from Nazareth to Judaea (a journey she was to make again, down to Bethlehem, not many months later). Elizabeth was six months pregnant, and Mary had already been told by an angel to expect a child who extraordinarily would be called the Son of God (Luke 1:35). No wonder there was excitement. Even the baby in Elizabeth's womb got excited! (Luke 1:41).

What a significant time of sharing this must have been. Not only was there sharing at a simply human level between two mothers-to-be who were also relatives, but the whole occasion was impregnated with the divine. Elizabeth knew that the baby Mary would bear was her Lord and Saviour (Luke 1:43).

How many of our sharing moments are raised above the mundane by an awareness not only of God's presence but of His purposes being worked out even in our life circumstances? Is our conversation 'seasoned with salt' in this way? Is there another Person present? Do we talk only one-to-one or three-way? In short, does God come into our moments of sharing?

There was a home I used to visit which had a plaque on the wall that left a lasting impression on me. It said: 'Christ is the Head of this house, The Unseen Guest at every meal, The Silent Listener to every conversation'.

There has been a lot of sharing going on during our cancer journey – between ourselves as husband and wife thrust into this scenario so early in our marriage, within our respective families (Isabel's much more than mine), among friends and former colleagues – some believers, some not. But we have aimed to keep our Lord and Saviour in the forefront of our minds throughout, whether we make any explicit mention of Him or not.

This has been good for me, as I have never been too comfortable with sharing very private emotions, especially when being expected to do so. What I have also had to learn is that I should be prepared to receive counsel or spiritual encouragement from whoever offers it, which can be difficult having been in pastoral ministry for over forty years and therefore usually being the one giving it out to others. When someone shares a text of scripture with me, I am tempted to think to myself, 'Do they think I don't know that?' rather than taking it for myself and paying attention to it for what it is. Oh, the dangers of spiritual pride! Hear Mary's response to the angel's sharing: 'May your word to me be fulfilled' (Luke 1:38).

I have found this poem by Eddie Askew a good reflection of how I have felt:

I need you, Lord.
A safe refuge. A shelter.
I used to scorn that thought.
Shelters were for the weak, and I was strong.
But pride's not what it was,
That's changed too.
And who am I, when mountains shake
To stand out in the storm?
I head for cover with the rest.
Cold with shock.
Another of the walking wounded in the fight.
I need your reassurance.
The strength that comes from you.
Yet even you, Lord,
Come to me in different ways.
Speaking new words in unexpected moments.
Shaking what little complacency I have left. [1]

---

1. Eddie Askew *Many Voices, One Voice* (Brentford, Middlesex: The Leprosy Mission International, 1985) p.33

CHAPTER 11

Lessons from COVID

Isabel

There have been two 'Big Cs' in our journey – cancer and COVID. The COVID pandemic has intensified the challenge for us both. Although I had a very serious cancer (Stage 4, meaning it had already spread to other organs of my body), I always felt quite confident that the medical staff would do their utmost to keep me stable. But COVID seemed to be something out of control, the news peppered with increasingly alarming statistics first from China, then Italy, and then the UK. This was unsettling for me because I knew I had to remain well enough for my cancer treatment, particularly the chemotherapy, to continue. In fact, I found the day we went into lockdown worse than the day of my diagnosis.

During this time my condition has ebbed and flowed, causing me to change my funeral plans several times this past year, not because of COVID as such but because of what the cancer was doing to my body. As I write now, my body is very weak.

We have been attending church Sunday by Sunday online as the risk of mixing with people is too great. We are, however, glad to have had this blessing.

COVID also meant that many of my friends and even some of my family were not able to visit me, which I found very hard indeed. This also extended to my times in hospital, even well after lockdown was lifted, with only my husband allowed to visit, and then by appointment for just one hour in a day.

Viewing all this from the inside doesn't, of course, give us the whole picture. We do actually know that God is still in control and has purposes of which we are largely unaware. Very many people were simply overtaken and overwhelmed by the COVID invasion and unable to cope because they lacked any bigger picture. We are able to say with the psalmist:

Yet I am always with you;
you hold me by my right hand.
You guide me with your counsel,
and afterwards you will take me into glory.
Whom have I in heaven but you?
And earth has nothing I desire besides you.
My flesh and my heart may fail,
but God is the strength of my heart
and my portion for ever (Psalm 73:23-26).

Oliver

Pandemics are not new. Think, for example, of the Spanish flu pandemic of 1918 where it is estimated that some fifty million people died! Like COVID, that also lasted quite a long time. But there has been a 'pandemic' going on quite a bit longer than that, in fact for the bulk of human history, of which we rarely speak. It began in a paradise garden (see Genesis 3:1–19; Romans 5:12), has affected every person who ever lived (except one!), and is fatal. There has only ever been one cure, only ever one person who deals with the penalty of sin, and who covers my sin in the sight of a holy God. He came at Christmas. Why was he named Jesus? As we have already seen, 'Because he will save his people from their sins' (Mathew 1:21). Quite simply, 'Christ Jesus came into the world to save sinners' (1 Timothy 1:15).

You might think that you are not a sinner. In that case, you haven't heard the diagnosis! Thankfully, there is a remedy to be found in the only person ever to be without sin, of which I speak more in the next chapter.

When COVID arrived, Isabel was immuno-suppressed because of her cancer treatment, so the nurse in her attempted to school me in a hygiene regime that was new to me. Every surface within reach had to be scrupulously disinfected, and my hands constantly washed in anti-bacterial soap (while singing 'Happy Birthday' through – twice). The problem with sin, though, is that we cannot actually get rid of it, even if we live the most morally 'hygienic' of lives. 'Although you wash yourself with soap and use an abundance of cleansing powder, the stain of your guilt is still before me', declares the Sovereign LORD' (Jeremiah 2:22). The only way is through accepting the grace of Jesus, as the hymn *Jesus lover of my soul* so beautifully summarises:

Plenteous grace with thee is found,
grace to cover all my sin;
let the healing streams abound;
make and keep me pure within.
Thou of life the fountain art;
freely let me take of thee;
spring thou up within my heart,
rise to all eternity.
(Charles Wesley)[1]

---

1. *Jesus, Lover of My Soul*, Sourced from www.hymnal.net/en/hymn/h/1057

CHAPTER 12

Purpose

Hold thou thy cross before my closing eyes
Shine through the gloom and point me to the skies
Heaven's morning breaks and earth's vain shadows flee;
In life, in death, O Lord, abide with me.
(Henry Francis Lyte)[1]

Oliver

Sadly, Isabel died before she could contribute to this final chapter. Even the previous few chapters she had to dictate to me as she was unable to write them down for herself. We had, however, made notes about what she wanted to say here. Here they are, exactly as we wrote them:

What *is* life?
– Eternal life is a reality
– Life is more than 'things'
– Life is more than time on earth

Bitterness at life cut short – what about Jesus at thirty-three?
Plans not realised – accepting that
Being content in every situation… this is something increasingly learned as cancer progresses.

---

1. *Abide With Me* sourced from hymnary.org/text/abide_with_me_fast_falls_the_eventide

I find myself writing this just a few days after a most memorable Thanksgiving Service for Isabel's life, which was attended by some 400 people (with an additional several hundred viewing online). This is testimony enough to the impact Isabel had upon so many lives. (A copy of the 'Reflections' part of that service describing Isabel's life is to be found in Appendix 1.) Immediately prior to that service, just close family and friends had gathered for the burial of Isabel's body in a cemetery close to our home in a beautiful spot overlooking the same stretch of water that she had been able to see throughout her illness from our bedroom window.

So, we are left with the question, 'Was there any purpose in all of this suffering?'

In truth, we may as well ask what was the purpose in Jesus dying at the tender age of thirty-three? Answer that question, and you will have discovered the pearl of great price (Matt. 13:45–46), the very key to the deep mysteries of life as it is.

We have already considered some prophetic words spoken at the time of His birth, such as the aged Simeon's prophecy to Jesus' mother Mary that a sword would pierce her soul (Luke 2: 35). There is a famous painting by Holman Hunt of Jesus as a young man in his father Joseph's carpentry shop with the shadow of a cross on the wall behind Him. There is an even more striking painting by an anonymous artist of Jesus as a small infant in His father's workshop. He is holding a rough nail in his hand, and there is the shadow of a cross on the floor behind Him. The whole of Jesus' life was preliminary and preparatory to His death on a cross. Why?

As I have said, to answer that is to find the solution to the riddle of life and to discover what lies at the heart of the universe – the love of God for fallen humankind. Someone has perceptively described Isabel as 'a life-giver' (literally in rescuing the lives of premature and very sick babies, but emotionally to everyone she met). Her life was but a faint reflection of God the life-giver. And His motivation is love (see John 3:16; 1 John 3:16; 1 John 4:10). It is the love of God that is at the heart of the universe. A dear friend of mine wrote in some meditations on Psalm 23:

> Love is not an impersonal force. It does not act randomly; there is no chance involved. It is personal. It is eternal. It is the very character of God Himself...

That love should be the Lord of your life. That love will be your guide, your shepherd; no matter what happens, nothing can separate you from such love.[2]

Those who live dependent on and safe in this love know that there is purpose, even in suffering the ravages of cancer. God had and still has a purpose enshrined in our story. For a start, it was surely purpose enough that the Thanksgiving Service had such an impact on the future lives of so many attending. And looking back over this journey, we learned the power of love between the two of us, a love stronger than death. I wrote these words to go with the wreath that is placed on Isabel's grave: 'To my darling Isabel Forever love Mr V'. But what is the true 'forever love'? It is the love of God for my soul, which is found in the ultimate demonstration at the cross where God Himself laid down His life for me. There is no greater love in the whole universe than this!

Let me tell you about the power of love. During the final weeks of Isabel's cancer journey, her twin sister, Margaret, came and stayed at our house to help care for Isabel. I am loathe to describe in detail what this involved; suffice to say that it was the most demanding of challenges. Margaret refused to leave the house and often went without sleep, so focused was she on caring for her sister right to the very end of the journey. Why? She loved her. And why was I prepared to do the same, working hand in glove with Margaret? Because I loved her too. (We jokingly called ourselves 'Nurse Nancy' and 'Dr Kildare'.)

We are told of Jesus, aware that the cross awaited Him, that 'having loved His own who were in the world, He loved them to the end' (John 13:1). Some of the old hymn writers wonderfully captured this love in their poetry. You could do worse than look up the section on His crucifixion and death in a hymn book or search online something like 'hymn love of Jesus' or 'hymn cross of Jesus'. You may find the hymn *O love, that wilt not let me go?* whose closing verses are:

2. Murray Watts, *Anthem for Life* (Farnham, Surrey: Waverley Abbey Resources, 2021) p 12

O Joy that seekest me through pain,
I cannot close my heart to thee.
I trace the rainbow through the rain,
and feel the promise is not vain,
that morn shall tearless be.

O Cross, that liftest up my head,
I dare not ask to fly from Thee;
I lay in dust life's glory dead,
And from the ground there blossoms red
Life that shall endless be.
(George Matheson)[3]

These were the words running through my head as we stood at Isabel's graveside and committed her severely broken body 'to the earth, ashes to ashes, dust to dust, in sure and certain hope of the resurrection to eternal life through our Lord Jesus Christ'.

If you would know true hope in the midst of grief and pain, dear reader, start at the cross. Hide your life in Christ and His love, then let your journey, whatever that may entail of joy or sadness, culminate in resurrection at the last day.

I write these words in the grip of grief, just a few months into bereavement. It was at this same stage in his own loss of his wife that C.S. Lewis described his grief like this: 'Her absence is like the sky, spread over everything.'[4] With this description my present emotions readily identify. These words also serve to point me to a higher and brighter sky covering us in life and in death – God's canopy of grace.

During Isabel's illness she was given a book of poems by a friend. One of these speaks very much to me just now:

---

3. Sourced from www.hymnal.net/en/hymn/h/432

4. C.S. Lewis, *A Grief Observed* (London: Faber and Faber, first published 1962, paperback edition 2013) p. 12

Just for a moment

Just for a moment
She is out of your sight.
You are under a cloud
She is now in the Light.

Just for a moment
You can't hear her voice
Though she is singing with angels
"Safe home!" they rejoice

Just for a moment
Your ways had to part
Though for ever you'll carry her
Deep in your heart.

Just for a moment
You blink back the tears.
Now she knows true freedom
From all pain and fears.

Just for a moment
Your life seems despoiled
Yet some day together
You'll share joy unalloyed.[5]

---

5. Fiona Sarjeant, *Heart to Heart* (Inverness: For the Right Reasons, 2012)

Reflections taken from the Thanksgiving Service for Isabel, which took place on 22 November 2021

These are words taken directly from the service and were compiled by Isabel's twin sister, Margaret.

All of us here today who had the enormous privilege of knowing Isabel, whether for a few years or many decades, were so blessed and enriched by having her in our lives and she's sorely missed.

Isabel Anne Seaton was born on 23 November 1961, twenty minutes ahead of her twin sister, Margaret. Their brother, Hamish, born three years later, completed the red-haired trio, and the family lived at Breadalbane, Grimsay, North Uist. Her mother, Margaret, a teacher, belonged to the island; her father, Donald, an agricultural advisor, was from Perthshire.

Her father's unexpected death, when she was six years old, had a huge impact on Isabel's outlook on life and death. For Isabel, knowing her mum was never bitter or angry with God over her father's death at a young age, was to be influential in how she and her family dealt with the prospect of dying and even more so in the light of her illness.

Isabel was influenced by growing up in a Christian home. Later when the family moved to Inverness in her teenage years, her church's youth fellowship and church camps were instrumental in forming her own personal relationship with her Saviour Jesus and developing her own personal faith. On the day of her diagnosis, Isabel said she wanted her life to be a witness to whoever she met on her cancer journey, showing her strength was coming from the Lord.

On leaving school, Isabel spent some months as an auxiliary at Raigmore Hospital, prior to commencing her general nursing training at the Western Infirmary, Glasgow. This was followed by midwifery training at Rottenrow Maternity Hospital. She subsequently became a nursing sister in Rutherglen and Rottenrow, prior to her appointment as an Advance Neo-Natal Nurse Practitioner in Raigmore in 2001, until her retirement in 2019.

She used to say her three priorities were her family, friends, and faith. Her family meant the world to her. She adored and massively respected her mum, Margaret, and her siblings, Margaret and Hamish. She loved talking about them, as well as Douglas and Carol, and no visit with Isabel would pass without her sharing some family story or incident.

She was very proud of each of her 'Fab Four', Rhona, Andrew, Eilidh and Calum, and loved being an auntie to them. She loved them as her own, spoilt them, encouraged them, cared for them and had a ball with them, while their weary parents looked forward to the break Auntie Belle's arrival gave. They lovingly thought of her as their third parent. She proudly gave Dr Eilidh her stethoscope on her retiral, and Andrew's first driving lesson was from Isabel on a very windy Uist beach!

Isabel was always so thankful to Margaret and Douglas, Hamish and Carol for sharing their children with her.

Isabel's love for her family ran so very deep. Following her diagnosis, the pain that she felt in those early days was such that she thought her 'heart would break into many tiny pieces' as she saw the effect it was having on her nearest and dearest.

The diagnosis with Stage 4 bowel cancer was immediately followed by surgery and aggressive treatment. Isabel just got on with it; she never ever complained. She wanted to ease the effects of her illness on the family. She was always so thankful for all that was being done for her and was such an example of grace and determination to us all. Throughout her diagnosis and illness, her concern continued to be for the family. After being critically ill eighteen weeks before her death, she put arrangements in place for her funeral to make it easier for everyone. She then organised a family photo shoot; she was insistent through her illness that they were making happy memories together.

She was always unfailingly glamorous and stunning. Even as a young girl she always had beads, a handbag over her arm, and a ribbon in her beautiful, curly red hair. Her sense of style continued – just the right coloured scarf or chosen necklace to set off an outfit. Her wardrobe was readily shared with whoever needed a dress or hat for a special occasion. Even in the later days of her illness she would carefully choose her outfit, complete with matching earrings and her Jo Malone perfume.

Isabel was the eldest child, the big sister who throughout her life without question loved and cared for her mum, her siblings, and their families. Her love and care for her family was shown in every detail of her life with them.

Family memories of her are vast, too many to recount here. From her quick responses as a little girl grabbing Hamish's pram as it rolled away with him... her unique twin bond with Margaret... regular trips to London with Margaret to participate in the Twin UK studies at St Thomas Hospital... fitting in a West End Show and shopping trip... to dropping everything to come and help them with new babies; nothing was ever too much trouble for her to do for her family.

Jetting off to Malaysia and Dubai to see Hamish and Carol or scooting down the motorways to visit Margaret and Douglas in England was no hardship for her. She delighted in the friendships with her siblings and Carol and Douglas.

Isabel was the organiser.... be it a family birthday meal, a trip away or a gift, it was organised efficiently, tastefully... just perfect in every way! She was our 'go to' for advice... Let's see what Isabel thinks we should do about this?

If we had an ache or a twinge, Isabel would always query it, such was her love for her family. In the week before her death, she continued to be concerned about Calum's health; when speaking was too difficult for her, she tapped his chest to show this. She was so pleased hearing that Rhona was returning to work in Scotland, saying it would be such a comfort to the family to have her nearer after her death.

Along with Isabel's care and devotion came Isabel's extravagant generosity and self-sacrifice. Whether letting Hamish, when a student, share her flat, her car, and her fridge or arriving at their homes with armfuls of flowers and goodies to eat..... or having her Fab 4 stay overnight in Inverness and run them to their work in the early morning... Isabel gave lavishly to family and others – of her love, her time, her talents, and her possessions.

Enjoying adventures together Isabel spent much time with her mum, treating her to the best of everything. Isabel had throughout her working life thought that she would spend her retirement further helping her mum. Although cancer intervened, Isabel's bond with her mum and the family grew deeper and stronger through her cancer journey. When asked on one occasion how she was feeling, she answered, 'a little bit sore and a very big bit sad' at the thought of leaving her dearest Oliver and her beloved family.

Her family relations held a special place for her. It was her delight to introduce Oliver to her North Uist roots and her Seaton relatives. Visiting her aunts and uncles on regular occasions... sharing passion for travel, walks, meals, and recounting stories from childhood, Isabel is remembered by her cousins as hospitable and caring, concerned about their health, one who valued family connections and went out of her way to help them, often in times of distress and their greatest need.

Isabel had the most amazing capacity and zest for life. She was like a whirlwind, effortlessly balancing all sorts of interests, friendships, and commitments. She loved being active: for many years she took part in all sorts of physical challenges across the Highlands. Rarely doing these on her own, she persuaded all sorts of couch-potato friends to join her in the Etape, the Highland Cross, or some other of her escapades.

She had a sense of adventure and loved travelling. The more remote and exotic the place, the more she loved it, from exploring Machu Picchu in Peru, to climbing Mount Kinabalu in Borneo, to attending a wedding in India, she never turned down an opportunity to visit somewhere she'd not been before. Always reading up well in advance about her destination, she was never fazed by new situations; in fact, she relished them and took them completely in her stride.

The defining characteristic about Isabel is that she loved people. She thrived on building and maintaining friendships with a whole range of people literally all over the world and was the most kind, generous, faithful, thoughtful friend.

As a young nurse, she shared a flat in Kersland Street, Glasgow with Margaret and three other girls. They all went their different ways afterwards, but Isabel was the one that always knew where they were in the world and what they were doing, as she faithfully maintained contact.

She would arrive at friends' houses and effortlessly slot into family life and enhance it so much. She embraced the children of her friends and harassed young mums would be thankful for the arrival of 'Mary Poppins' to sort out the family. If there was a red-headed child in the family all the better – Isabel loved her fellow reds! One friend says she always used to wonder what people did without an 'Isabel' in their lives. She was such a blessing and help to many in countless ways.

Friends with sick babies recall she was always on hand to reassure, whether that entailed travelling to Glasgow for the day or speaking for an hour on the phone in the last weeks of her life.

Just before her cancer was diagnosed, when she wasn't feeling well at all, she still dropped everything to support a friend on the West Coast who had just been bereaved. Such was Isabel's selflessness and her loyalty to her friends.

She was naturally hospitable and had an irrepressible desire to have people round to her home. She effortlessly loved to cook the most delicious food for them and could literally chat all day.

At church she provided home baking and meals. She once said that it was part of her service to invite groups of people regularly to her home to feed them and help them to meet and connect with others. What a huge blessing this was! And she was fun to be around and drew people in with her friendly warm ways. She lived out Jesus' commandment, 'Love each other as I have loved you' ... and what a privilege it has been to be loved by her.

Colleagues recall wonderful memories of Isabel, or Izzy, at work, in both Glasgow and Inverness. With her positivity and 'can do' attitude, if there was a very sick baby and everyone was running about, you know you could rely on her. Trusting her calm demeanour, skills and judgement, staff felt very safe. A nurse friend recalls they wanted to be a nurse 'just like Isabel'. She had a shining, humble joy that illuminated the places she worked.

She combined a thorough, reliable expertise with a deep kindness and compassion for the babies and their families. Her care of babies included ward rounds in SCBU[1], baby checks in the postnatal ward, and resuscitations in labour ward and theatre.

This kindness and compassion also extended to her colleagues in the team. Colleagues remember she was fun to be around, always elegant and stylish – the ANNP (Advanced Neo-Natal Practitioner) office mirror is still fondly known as Isabel's lipstick mirror – always positive, thoughtful about others, generous to all, full of stories and interesting conversation.

Isabel gave her time in teaching midwives, junior doctors, and medical students over many years, patiently passing on her knowledge and skills in a way that encouraged those she was teaching.

With her colleagues a strong trio of ANNPs were formed, supporting one another, helping to move the neo-natal service forward as they taught neo-natal care across the Highlands. Her work involved transferring babies across the country. Margaret once received a very welcome and unexpected phone-call.... Isabel was landing at Cambridge airport with a baby and could she meet her and bring sandwiches for her colleagues.

The deep sadness felt at her passing is balanced by the knowledge that she is now with the Lord Jesus, who she followed so faithfully and well.

In her church life, Isabel's wonderful affirming presence and ministry of service covered a huge number of activities, touching many people's lives since her arrival at CCC (Culduthel Christian Centre, Inverness) twenty plus years ago.

From creche co-ordinator to Ladies Ministry Team to Blythswood fundraising and shoebox sorting days and delivering them to Romania, to coffeeshop volunteering, to quiet one-to-one study with someone eager to understand the Bible, to actively participating in homegroups and a

---

1. This stands for Special Care Baby Unit

prayer triplet, to being on the Welcome and Greeting team and serving coffee/teas at the hatch, to providing many meals, to encouraging our physical health through the CCC cycling group, and helping at Alpha. This list is not exhaustive!

She had a love for all ages within the fellowship and used her gifts to create times to quietly encourage and build up others. The bonds formed while mentoring young people became so evident in the years of her illness as so many of them continued a close relationship with her.

Isabel's combined passions were obvious with her interest and commitment to Wakisa Ministries in Kampala Uganda, a Crisis Pregnancy Care Centre for young girls and their babies. On both her visits Isabel effortlessly came alongside the teenage mums, gained their confidence, quickly noted what could be done to provide better care and supplied both practical and professional help.

In all her involvements she did so cheerfully, inclusively, caring deeply for people and showing Jesus' love and concern to everyone she met, as she humbly pointed others to her Saviour.

Isabel's marriage to Oliver was a big life-changing event just over three years ago. She was so overjoyed to have met her soulmate, with many shared interests and hopes for serving Christ together at home and abroad. The ministry they envisaged was not to be, but we believe an even greater ministry glorifying God was unfolding through her illness. Oliver so calmly and selflessly loved and cared for Isabel during her illness. At every turn he was a steadying and strengthening influence and was the most wonderful blessing to Isabel and to her family. A true gift from God! Isabel did not see that they were to be pitied by seemingly thwarted plans at the start of their marriage, but they were completely reassured that they were at the centre of God's will for them. As she said, they were trusting an unknown future to a known God.

Having put together a video describing their experiences, which "connected" with so many who have watched it, an idea of a booklet to connect with a similar audience emerged. A motto which Isabel and Oliver had throughout their cancer journey was 'Living with cancer, walking with God'. This underpins the subject of the booklet, and Isabel was able to complete most of her part of the book before she died.

Isabel's cancer journey was complicated by the COVID pandemic. Limited face-to-face contact with family and friends was so painful for her, and our hearts ached with hers at not seeing her. She bravely attended her fortnightly chemo treatment, knowing the risks that COVID infection could pose to her compromised immune system. She and we are so thankful that this service continued during the incredible pressures on the NHS.

We marvelled at Isabel in so many ways during her life and will continue to do so even after her death. She was dearly treasured by so many but what was the key to her care and compassion, her willingness to put others' needs before her own, her desire to open her home and to give herself so unstintingly to others? The answer is in her deep Christian faith. She loved Jesus Christ as her Lord and Saviour, and since He gave himself for others and put their needs before His own, and commanded His followers to do the same, so Isabel sought to do likewise. That was her big priority, and in these latter years she became more and more convicted of the importance of sharing the Good News about Jesus with others who didn't yet know Him.

Isabel died on 4 November 2021, taken not we believe 'by the cruel hand of fate but by the gentle hand of God'.

Oliver

Following Isabel's diagnosis of Stage 4 bowel cancer so soon after our marriage and retirement, her concern was for others. She did not complain but was thankful for all the medical treatment and support she had received. Shortly before her death she held up her hands drawing a circle shape and said, 'Thank everyone'.

We do most gratefully thank: The Radiology Dept, The Colo-Rectal Team and The Chemotherapy Unit at Raigmore Hospital, The Munlochy GP Practice, Marie Curie Services, our MacMillan Nurse, and The Dingwall District Nurses for their treatment and care of Isabel and for the compassion and dignity which they gave her.

We also thank friends, family, and our church families for their prayerful and practical care.

What can I say at a time like this? I'm struggling for words. Cancer is a truly terrible disease, but it did draw Isabel and myself so very close these past three years and served to focus us on walking this painful journey with God, knowing that 'His purposes will ripen fast / Unfolding every hour / The bud may have a bitter taste / But sweet will be the flower.'[2]

Our love for one another ran deep, but never as deep as the love of Jesus for her soul and mine. Jesus, in whose arms she now rests. Isabel radiated this love and many of you here today have been touched and blessed by this, haven't you? And her life will continue to speak to us for many a year hence, won't it?

NB A video recording of the entire Thanksgiving Service can be viewed online at: youtu.be/DiO-5aG_zYk

---

2. *God Moves in a Mysterious Way*, sourced from hymnary.org/text/god_moves_in_a _mysterious_way Accessed April 2022

Transcript of Video Testimony first played at Culduthel Christian Centre

Sunday 31 May 2020

Oliver

COVID-19 has come as a shock to all of us with its unprecedented effects on our lives. There is talk now of 'a new normal'. What makes our story a bit out of the ordinary is that cancer came into our life as a huge shock just four months into our marriage with the words 'in sickness and in health' still ringing in our ears. So, this was now our 'new normal'! We have developed a simple motto to express this: 'Living with cancer, walking with God.'

Certain texts and hymns became special. I recall that early on we sang together at the piano: *When I fear my faith will fail / He will hold me fast.*

Isabel

A cancer diagnosis was made quickly, and I was given the news it had spread to many of my organs. This was a huge shock, as I thought I was very fit and healthy. I decided from that moment on not to be bitter but to be thankful for the life I had lived. And thankful for my amazing family, friends, church family, and work colleagues.

Though the whirl of emotions was very intense, knowing what was ahead, I had complete trust in an amazing surgical team but more importantly trusted God for the way ahead – on most days.

Reading *Jesus Calling* by Sarah Young, many verses from the Bible really spoke to me in these early days, such as Isaiah 41:10 'So do not fear, for I am with you; do not be dismayed, for I am your God. I will strengthen you and help you; I will uphold you with my righteous right hand.'

To know God was guarding over me during the days and especially the nights at that time was a huge comfort. The porter wheeling me along the corridor to theatre said that he had never seen anyone so calm. Two of my friends had popped by just before to help put my TED stockings on and then prayed me into theatre. What a blessing and special time that was – and how safe I felt in God's arms that afternoon.

The one thing that was high up for me was to ensure that my faith, which I talked about at work and with friends when I was well, would remain steadfast and sure and that God would receive the glory. God through His Holy Spirit showered us with strength.

I was due to retire five days after my diagnosis and my leaving do was being organised (soon to be cancelled). Two further leaving dos were also aborted. But in the middle of February this year we plumped for a date in the middle of March. So, thirteen months after leaving work, I had a very special leaving do. I was very aware that God wanted me to say that He was sustaining us, that my future was and still is uncertain on this earth, but I really wasn't sure how I could get this across to them. Three weeks before I had come across a podcast from Jeremy Marshall, a London banker and a Christian, who was diagnosed initially with a curable cancer but progressing to incurable cancer. He was forty-nine years old. He chronicled his journey in his book *Beyond the Big C: Hope in the face of death*. I then decided that I would buy fifty books and give one to each person who came to my do. I prayed that even if my friends didn't want to read the book, they might pass it on to someone else who might find it helpful. I am so thankful for that opportunity.

Less than two weeks later we decided to isolate and shield, and the opportunity to share my faith with my colleagues with a cancer diagnosis might never have happened. I now know why my do didn't take place earlier. I feel it was good that they received this book just prior to the COVID-19 outbreak. Truly perfect timing, I believe.

Oliver

Words which have meant a lot to us during this time we have stuck to our fridge door, including these:

There is a hope that lifts my weary head
A consolation strong against despair
That when the world has plunged me in its deepest pit
I find the Saviour there
Through present sufferings future's fear
He whispers courage in my ear
For I am safe in everlasting arms
And they will lead me home.

One of my favourite verses is the words of Job in chapter 23: 'He knows the way that I take' – that *we* take!

God is calling us to walk this way together. It has meant huge challenges for both of us, but it has undoubtedly drawn us closer together and to God.

Isabel

Each day since diagnosis I waken to Bible verses from friends, house group, and prayer triplets as we face another day. The message I received on 9 March just after the do was Proverbs 3:5, 'Trust in the LORD with all your heart and lean not on your own understanding.' We could feel fearful with all the illness and COVID on its way, but God is infinite, and I am not. But what I realised was that Jesus was carrying me through, through silent and spoken prayer, and the key for us was to start each day in communication with Him and to communicate frequently through the day with Him.

Although all this sounds that there have been no struggles – there have! Shortly after my chemo started, I woke one morning sobbing wondering how I would get through the day and was straight away reminded of Joseph in the pit. Now I have read that story of Joseph many times, but that day I felt it was me at the bottom of that pit with no way out. I felt so far from God that morning that I could not communicate with Him, but then of course realised that He had not abandoned me. On a trip to Israel a couple of years ago we visited Masada where Angus explained that the pit/cistern that Joseph was in was like this one – massive boulders on either side making it extremely difficult to climb out of. I then felt I understood the agony Joseph was in that day.

1 John 3:2 reminds us that God has already taken every step necessary to bring us the ultimate encouragement, namely His presence in our hearts now and eternal life with Him in heaven.

Before I finish, I just want to leave you with this quote from Joni Eareckson Tada commenting on the Joseph incident: 'Problems are real and I'm not denying that suffering hurts. I'm just denying that it matters in the grander scheme of things. It is light and momentary compared with what our response is producing for us in heaven. The Lord inferred that if His followers were to share in His glory they would also have to share in His sufferings.'

Oliver

I've had a feeling many times of being unable to really help – especially medically! And yet I know that God has placed me here for a purpose – 'for such a time as this'.

'My heart and my flesh may fail, but God is the strength of my heart and my portion for ever' (Ps. 73:26).

Suffering/trials are mysterious! We don't ask for an *explanation* but rather in all of this we look for a *revelation*. After all his trials, Job was able to say, 'Now my eyes have seen You' (Job 42:5).

NB A video recording of the video testimony can be viewed online at: youtu.be/mHQCXLNSLI8

Acknowledgements

The authors wish to thank Waverley Abbey Resources for their ready acceptance of this book for publishing and for their warmth, encouragement and professional help throughout the preparation of the manuscript for print.

Learn to be the Difference

We help people to develop their gifts, be equipped and make a difference.

We provide training in the areas of

- **Counselling**
- **Leadership**
- **Spiritual Formation**
- **Chaplaincy**

Courses that equip you to be the difference

Lightning Source UK Ltd.
Milton Keynes UK
UKHW020018150922
408867UK00012B/1459